of urban living

Standardisation of parts

Rationalisation of process and methods

Modern industrial design based on
the principle of conspicuous economy

Founding principles of the Isokon company, 1929

ISOKON GALLERY

THE STORY OF A NEW VISION OF URBAN LIVING

The Isokon Gallery
Lawn Road
Hampstead
London NW3 2XD

isokongallery.org

Text authors
John Allan
Elizabeth Darling
Jyri Kermik
Fiona MacCarthy
Jill Pearlman
Alan Powers
Christopher Wilk

Exhibition team
John Allan
Tom de Gay
Magnus Englund
Sol Kawage
Fiona Lamb
Gjøril Reinecke

Book design by Tom de Gay

Catalogue © Isokon Gallery Trust
Texts © the authors

First published by the Isokon Gallery Trust in 2016
Second edition published in 2021
ISBN 978-1-5262-0354-0

The Isokon Gallery Trust is a not-for-profit charity regulated by the Charity Commission and registered as a Charitable Incorporated Organisation,
№ 1161069

The Isokon Gallery Trust has made every effort to contact copyright holders of images; they will be happy to correct in subsequent editions any errors or omissions which are brought to their attention.

All rights reserved. No part of this book may be reprinted, reproduced, transmitted or utilised in any form or by any electronic, mechanical or other means, now known or hereafter invented, including photocopying and recording, or in any information storage and retrieval system, without permission in writing of the copyright holders and of the publishers.

Contents

Introduction	2
Jack & Molly Pritchard The clients Fiona MacCarthy	10
Wells Coates The architect Elizabeth Darling	16
The Isokon Origins & design Elizabeth Darling	25
The Bauhaus and Isokon Christopher Wilk	38
Venesta The plywood Jyri Kermik	42
Isokon The furniture Christopher Wilk	48
The Isobar The social hub John Allan	60
Hampstead in the 1930s Alan Powers	68
A hotbed of spies The secret history Jill Pearlman	74
Ruin & rescue The restoration John Allan	78
Chronology	88
Further reading	89
Image credits	90
Sponsors	91

Introduction

The Isokon Gallery tells the remarkable story of the Isokon building, also known as Lawn Road Flats, the pioneering modern apartment block opened in 1934 as a progressive experiment in new ways of urban living.

Commissioned by champions of modern design Jack and Molly Pritchard and designed by Wells Coates, Isokon was home to Bauhaus émigrés, artists, authors and architects – and even a number of Soviet spies.

The Isokon company also pioneered bent plywood furniture, and classic designs by Marcel Breuer, Egon Riss and Ernest Race form part of the exhibition.

The gallery also relates the story of the building's recent and dramatic rescue after years of post-war decline and features original spaces and fittings salvaged from the derelict shell during the restoration.

Jack and Molly Pritchard
the clients

Wells Coates
the architect

Dressing room and kitchen reconstructed in the gallery space from original fittings salvaged in the 2004 refurbishment

Molly and Jack, with sons Jonathan and Jeremy, on Isokon opening day, 9 July 1934

Jack & Molly Pritchard
The clients

Fiona MacCarthy

Lawn Road Flats are the visionary concept of a remarkable couple, Jack and Molly Pritchard. Both came from solid professional middle class families but they were true progressives in their outlook. Lawn Road Flats were not only architecturally innovative but they were socially experimental too.

A new way of living

Lawn Road Flats were conceived by Jack and Molly Pritchard, who married in 1924, as a bid for freedom from the middle class conventions in which they had been brought up.

> How do we want to live? What sort of framework must we build around ourselves to make that living as pleasant as possible?

These were basic questions asked by Molly Pritchard in drawing up the brief for a new form of urban living for young London professionals. This ideal form of life would be streamlined, anti-bourgeois, non-domestic, untrammelled by superfluous possessions and (up to a point) sexually liberated.

Jack & Molly

Jack and Molly Pritchard have come to be regarded as the archetypal Hampstead modern couple. Jack Craven Pritchard (1899–1992) was born at 6 Compayne Gardens, off the Finchley Road. The family soon afterwards moved to Maresfield Gardens. Jack's father was an up-and-coming barrister.

Molly Pritchard (1900–85) was born Rosemary Cooke. Her father was a London solicitor, her mother the daughter of the senior partner in her father's firm. Jack and Molly first met as undergraduates at Cambridge. Jack, having served in the Navy in the First World War, was at Pembroke college, reading engineering. Molly was at Girton, studying medicine. She was later to practise as a psychiatrist with modernist consulting rooms in Harley Street.

↑
Jack and Molly Pritchard, aged about fifteen

→
Walter Gropius, left, and Jack Pritchard at Gropius's 85th birthday, 18 May 1968

Continental connections

Jack Pritchard was well travelled and, more than most Englishmen of his generation, an admirer of modern European architecture. When working for Venesta Plywood Company he commissioned an exhibition stand from Le Corbusier. He was influenced by continental experiments in communal living in his ideas for Lawn Road Flats. Jack and Molly were believers in the free education movements of the 1930s, opening a nursery school in Hampstead managed by Beatrix Tudor-Hart, with whom Jack had a daughter, Jennifer. The Pritchards sent their own two children Jonathan and Jeremy to Dora Russell's notoriously experimental Beacon Hill school.

The Pritchards believed in good food, fine wine and vigorous uncensored conversation. The convivial atmosphere they created at Lawn Road Flats was unique in the Britain of that time. Here from the middle 1930s they provided a home from home for numerous refugees from Nazi Europe, among them Walter Gropius, founder of the Bauhaus.

Jack at Isokon, Blythburgh, 1970s

Urban living to rural retreat

After the war Jack Pritchard was appointed Director of the Furniture Development Company. He and Molly built a house named Isokon at Blythburgh in Suffolk to designs by Jack's daughter Jennifer and her architect husband Colin Jones. After selling Lawn Road Flats to the New Statesman newspaper in 1969 the Pritchards gravitated towards Blythburgh, entertaining their multitude of friends with continuing verve and generosity. Their iconoclastic outlook continued in old age.

Wells Coates
The architect

Elizabeth Darling

Lawn Road Flats marked a turning point in Coates's career. It was his first complete building and one which demonstrated his consummate skills as a designer of space and form.

Seeds of collaboration

Wells Coates (1895–1958) first came to the attention of the Pritchards through the pages of the design press. Articles showed the shop interior he had designed for the silk manufacturers Cryséde (later Cresta), in which he used plywood extensively in just the sort of manner that Jack was trying to promote as part of Venesta's programme to expand its market to the architectural profession. In March 1929, the company contacted Coates and not long after the two men met. The encounter sowed the seeds of the collaboration that, five years later, was manifested in the Lawn Road Flats.

Japan to Canada

Born in Tokyo to parents who were missionaries for the Canadian Methodist Church, Coates was educated privately by tutors, learning both traditional Japanese craft skills and the eminently modern practices of shorthand and typing. Leaving Japan in 1913, he sailed for Canada to enter university. His studies were interrupted by war service in the Canadian Field Artillery and the RAF, and it was not until 1922 that he completed a degree in Mechanical Engineering. Although this would have taught him the techniques of drawing plans and blueprints, and embedded in him a lifelong preoccupation with the mechanics of how things fit together and work, this was the only design education that Coates received. He had no formal training as an architect.

London transformation

Coates came to England in 1922 to study for a PhD, and was seemingly destined for an academic career. However, in an early sign of the progressiveness which chimed so well with that of the Pritchards, he rejected academia within weeks of being awarded his doctorate in 1924 and instead devoted the next four years to his transformation into a modern intellectual and writer (meanwhile supporting himself as a secretary and journalist).

> **As creative architects we are concerned with a Future which must be planned, rather than a Past which must be patched up.**
> Wells Coates, 1934

In the clubs, studios and bedsits of London's most avant-garde quarter of Fitzrovia, he came to understand the need to move ways of living, working, and creating away from outmoded norms, but it was only when he re-designed the rooms into which he and his new wife, Marion Grove, moved in 1928 that he realised his vocation was in architecture. He never looked back. Through his bohemian friends he gained the Cresta Silks commission, and began to develop a distinctive architectural language which combined the use of the most modern materials (like plywood) with a severe simplicity of form and compactness of planning.

Cresta Silks store, Brighton, 1930
with lettering by McKnight Kauffer

Isokon commission

It was this approach to design that seemed an answer to the Pritchards' disappointment with the first plans for the site on Lawn Road and they recruited him as their architect for a new scheme. Over the ensuing years, and after much debate and not a little disagreement, scheme gave way to scheme before it was agreed to build the block of minimum flats which was completed in the summer of 1934.

MARS and beyond

Over the rest of the decade he consolidated his reputation as a leading British modernist through his leadership of the MARS Group (the British branch of CIAM), his work as an industrial designer, especially for the electronics manufacturer EKCO, and as the architect of a series of further permutations on the Lawn Road model at Embassy Court (Brighton) and Palace Gate (west London).

After the war, Coates's most notable commission was for the Telekinema at the Festival of Britain (1951). In 1956, he settled permanently in Vancouver where he began to work with local architects on the redevelopment of its downtown area. The plans for this had only recently been announced when he died suddenly of a heart attack in June 1958.

→
Isokon design drawing,
Wells Coates, c.1934

↑
Wells Coates and his 1925 Lancia Lambda, 1956

←
The Wingsail Catamaran, 1948: a new kind of sailing boat to Coates's own design

→ AD 65 EKCO radio, 1934

↘ Embassy Court, 1935

This building... is perhaps the most modern building in England. It is not only modern as an architectural piece – it expresses a revolutionary idea for living.

Molly Pritchard, 1934

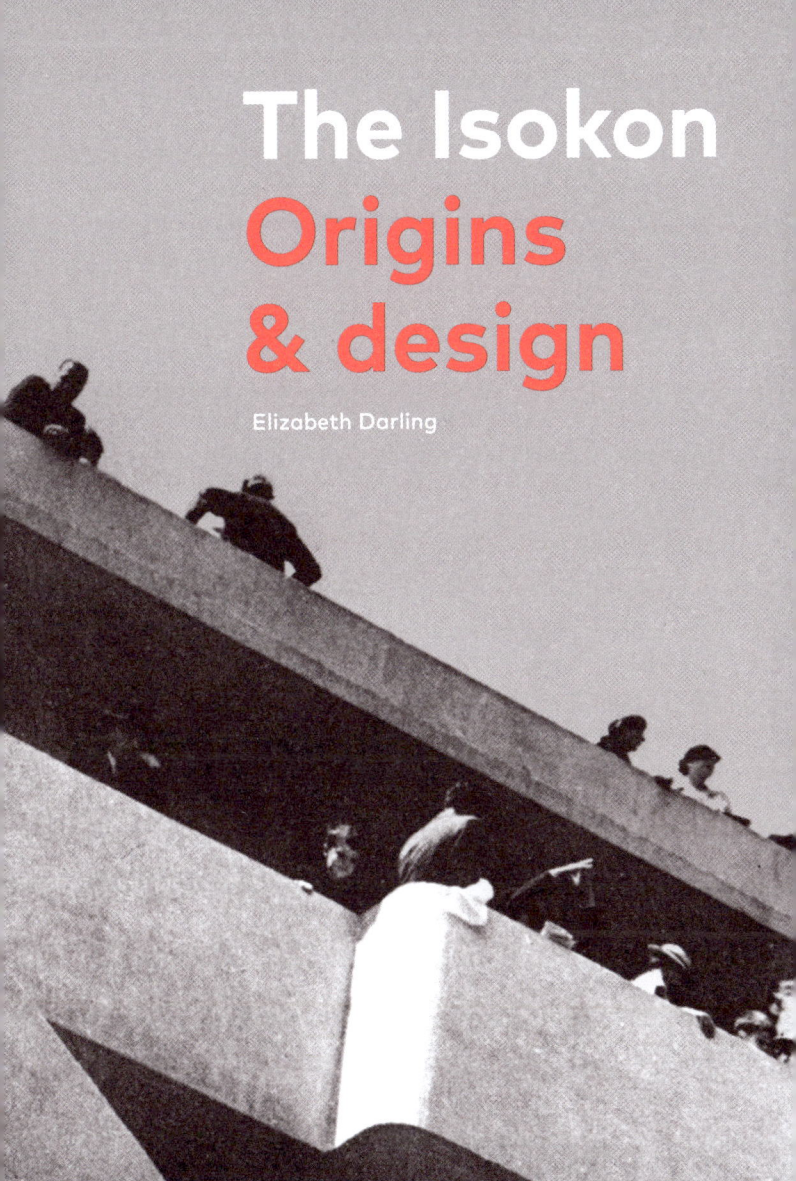
The Isokon
Origins & design

Elizabeth Darling

Origins

In 1929 Jack and Molly purchased a plot of land on Lawn Road on which to build a family house. A first design by Molly's sister and brother-in-law was commissioned but, in ways they could not quite articulate, was not right. It was at this moment that Coates's work first came to their attention; he was quickly recruited as their new architect. Over the next 18 months they embarked on a project to work out the best form of dwelling for their needs, reading widely and visiting continental European housing projects including the Weissenhof Siedlung. Coates promised his patrons:

> I can plan a house – a machine to live in – which will give you better accommodation than that provided by the present plan.

The initial results of this work were two schemes for houses. The first, dated March 1930, was for a single house, the second, in July, was for a pair of houses (one for the Pritchards, and one for Coates and his wife Marion who was about to give birth to their daughter) with a nursery. Neither came to fruition. Next, after the best part of a year's further debate and research, the trio embarked on a new, and highly ambitious plan. This was to take on the house building industry through the development of a series of mass-producible house-types – named Isotypes – constructed from a system of pre-made component parts, all designed by Coates.

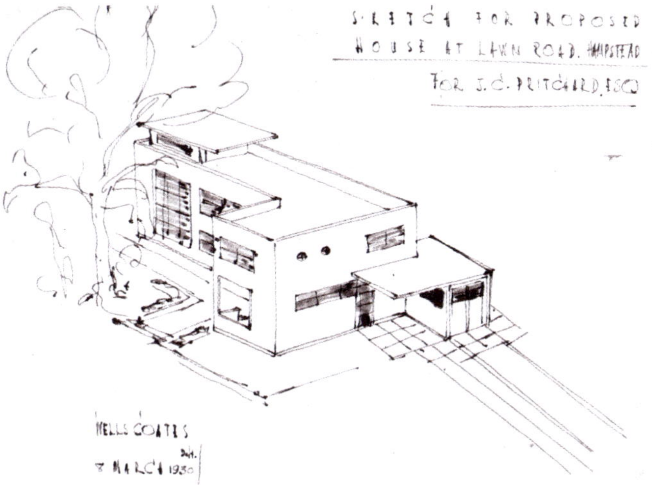

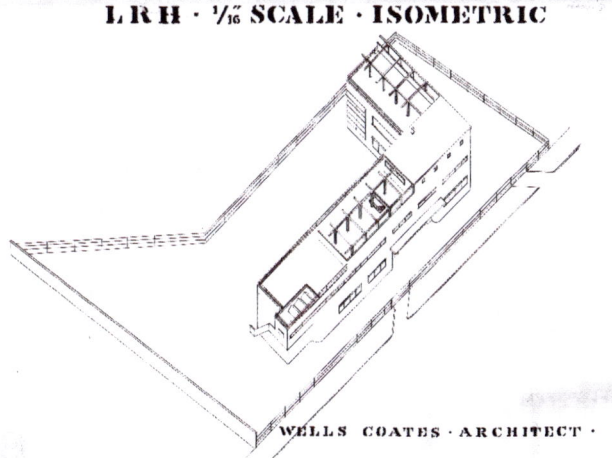

Initial designs for the Lawn Road site, 1930

Flat plan

In summer 1931, the fate of the Lawn Road site was decided. Instead of a house, the idea of a block of flats was proposed. The consensus was that this was the most appropriate, and modern, use of land for a city site – although whose idea it was proved a matter of much contention over the years to come. Molly would write to Coates in 1935:

> You accuse me of putting over the flat idea as mine – well so it was – I have felt you to be unkind when I have heard you put it over as yours – therefore the truth must be that, as a result of a germ dropped from you and another from me, the idea came to us both independently.

By December 1931, the Isokon Company was formed to develop the flats, the Isotypes (designed but never realised), and a range of plywood furniture. During 1932 the brief for the block was refined with flats to be of minimum dimensions comprising a main living space, compact bathroom, dressing room and kitchen. The target market was defined as 'businessmen and women who have no time for domestic troubles'. The Pritchard family would be accommodated in a penthouse. Financing for the scheme was assured following the exhibit of a prototype minimum flat at the Dorland Hall Exhibition of Industrial Art in the Home in June 1933. Tenders were sought in July 1933, and the budget set at £12,500. Work on site began in September, and the block was handed over on 26 June 1934 (at a final cost of £14,850).

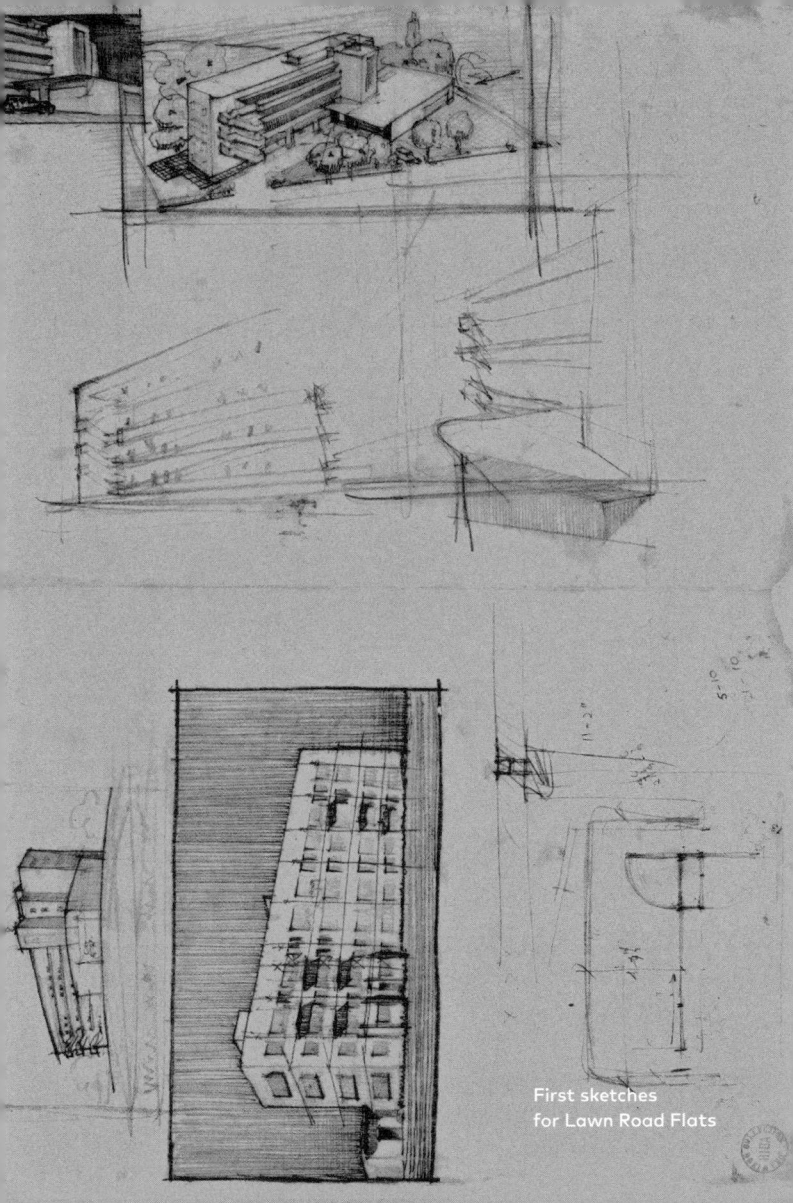

First sketches for Lawn Road Flats

Lawn Road Flats under construction, 1934

Design

The formal appearance of the block was derived from its structure. This was determined by the fact that two railway tunnels ran directly underneath each end of the site, requiring Coates to use a system of construction that could cantilever the extremities of the building over the tunnels. The solution was a monolithic reinforced concrete frame (its render tinted a light pink), Coates exploiting its properties to design the dramatically projecting access balconies on the Lawn Road front. The effortless modernity of the block formed a sharp contrast to the old-fashioned houses which surrounded it.

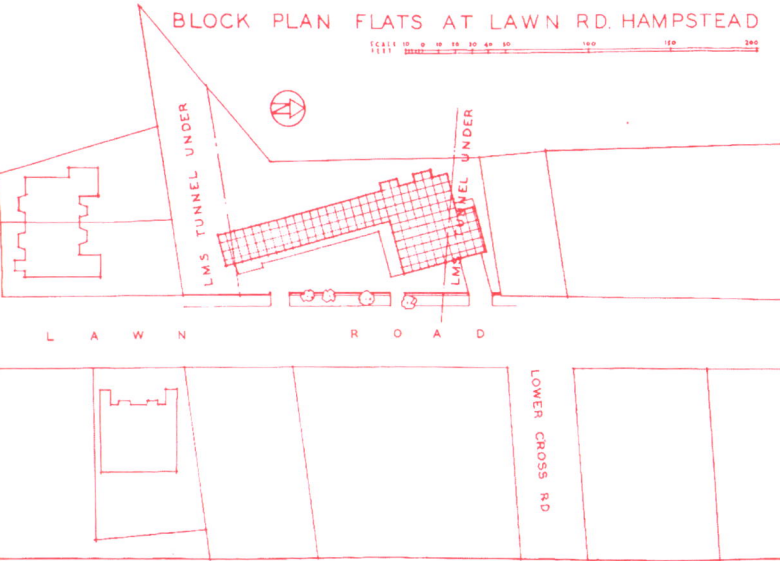

Accommodation

As originally built, the block comprised four, gallery-accessed storeys. The Pritchards' flat topped the block and comprised a main flat with smaller annex for their boys. Each floor contained a larger 'double' flat at the south end and from first to third floor level five standard minimum flats plus a double size studio flat entered next to the stairs and lift. At ground floor level were also three staff flats and a kitchen and laundry to serve the residents. These spaces were later converted into the Isobar by FRS Yorke and Marcel Breuer.

The Gropius's flat (no. 15), which had a dividing partition introduced on Ise's arrival, separating the introductory space from the bed area overlooking the nature reserve

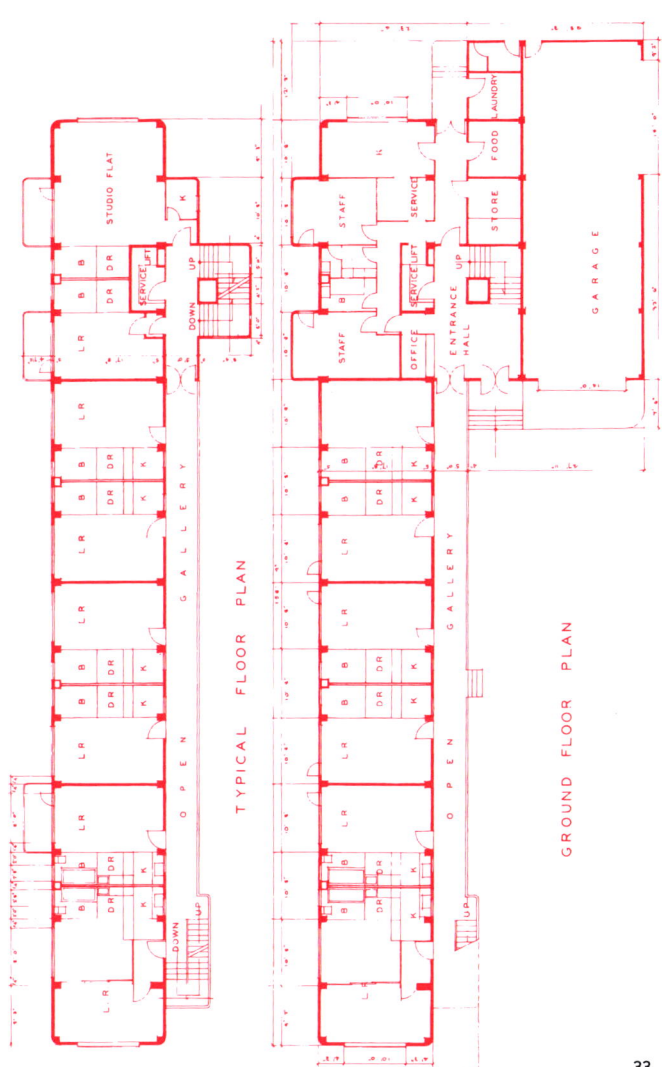

Minimum flat

The 'minimum' was the dominant flat-type. Its total dimensions were 5.4m × 4.67m with the main living area 5.4m × 3.15m. Built-in furniture demarcated the living and sleeping areas of the main room while sliding doors kept discreet the 'service' strip of rooms : dressing room, bathroom and a tiny electric kitchen, 1.4m × 1.52m, planned around the arm-reach of its user.

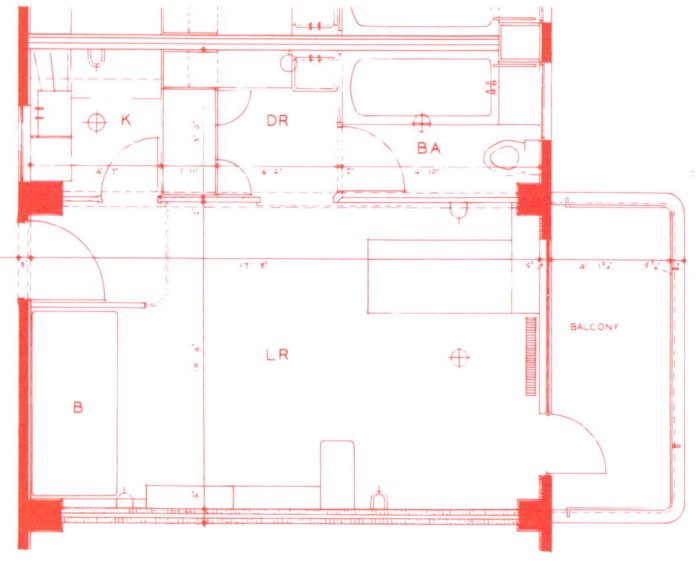

↑
Minimum flat plan, 1933

→
Minimum flat: living room with bed, dressing room, kitchen

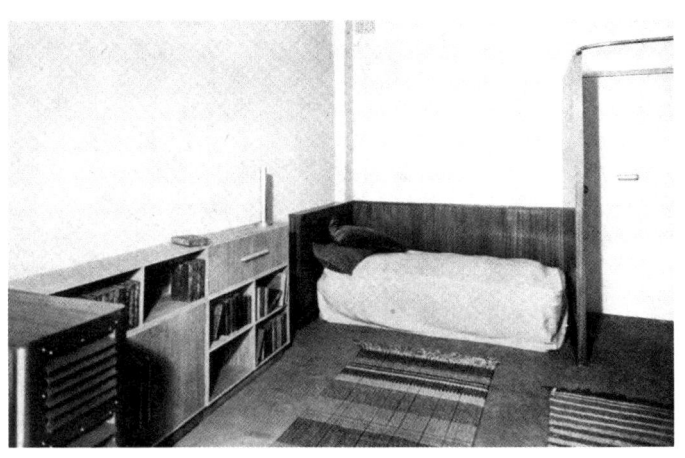

Launch

At the opening ceremony on 9 July 1934, Molly Pritchard reminded her guests of the importance of the block declaring: *This building... is perhaps the most modern building in England. It is not only modern as an architectural piece – it expresses a revolutionary idea for living.* A sentiment echoed in Gerald Barry's report in the News Chronicle a few days later:

The experiment is the signpost to a new order. It represents in concrete and steel the new attitude towards this business of living which is beginning to emerge from our present-day chaos.

→
Launching the Isokon with
a bottle of beer, 9 July 1934

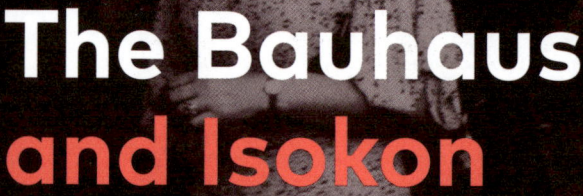

The Bauhaus and Isokon

Christopher Wilk

Jack Pritchard appointed Walter Gropius as Controller of Design at the Isokon Furniture Company, thus bringing the ideals and principles of the modernist school to London.

World View

The Bauhaus was the most influential art and design school of the twentieth century. It existed only from 1919–1933, most famously in the German city of Dessau, where it was housed in remarkable modernist buildings which looked, in part, like a glass and concrete factory. The founding Director of the Bauhaus was German architect Walter Gropius, a man Jack Pritchard described as *the leader of modern development in design* and someone he came to regard as a father figure.

In 1931 Pritchard visited the Bauhaus on a pilgrimage to see innovative contemporary architecture in Germany, though Gropius had resigned as Director in 1928 and the school was, in fact, closed during the visit.

→
Bauhaus Dessau building by Walter Gropius, 1926

←
First birthday party for Lawn Road Flats: Marcel Breuer (left) on the roof with Ise and Walter Gropius

Jack Pritchard saw in the idea of the Bauhaus a reflection of his own world view. He believed in progressive, non-traditional education and shared with the Bauhaus a belief that teaching began by exploring the very fundamentals not only of art but of life. He was attracted to the Bauhaus's strong belief in the transformative power of technology as well as its visual expression. He was also drawn to the school's technocratic, quasi-scientific rhetoric. Although Pritchard's knowledge of the Bauhaus was second-hand, it nonetheless stood, as it did for others interested in continental modernism, as a powerful symbol of a means by which to reinvent and improve the world.

←
Distinguished Bauhaus artist, designer and teacher László Moholy-Nagy designed advertising graphics for both Venesta and Isokon

→
Walter Gropius and Maxwell Fry, design for Isokon flats, St Leonard's Hill, Windsor, c.1935. Two blocks of 110 apartments, unbuilt.

The Bauhaus in Britain

Jack Pritchard was one of a group of British modernists working energetically in 1934 to enable Gropius to leave Nazi Germany by guaranteeing the architect employment in Britain. Pritchard's contribution was to offer him a place to live at Lawn Road Flats and, after his arrival, to offer him a job. The connections between the Bauhaus and Isokon were based on Jack Pritchard's sense of a spiritual and ideological kinship but also on the fact that four major Bauhaus teachers came to live at Lawn Road Flats: Walter Gropius, Marcel Breuer, László Moholy-Nagy and Naum Slutzky.

Walter Gropius arrived in 1934 and lived at Lawn Road until he left Britain for America in 1937. Starting in 1934, Pritchard involved Gropius and his English architectural partner Maxwell Fry in two schemes for blocks of Isokon flats, one in Manchester and one in Windsor. In 1936 additional flats and a restaurant near Lawn Road Flats were designed. None of these projects were built. Pritchard also appointed Gropius as the grandly titled Controller of Design at the Isokon Furniture Company. Pritchard came to regard his three years working with Gropius as having led to one of the most important relationships of his life and the two stayed in touch for the rest of Gropius's life.

Venesta
The plywood

Jyri Kermik

The furnishings in the Lawn Road Flats showcased the technological and aesthetic possibilities of plywood as part of Pritchard and Coates' pioneering architectural proposition.

Showcase

Between 1925 and 1935 Jack Pritchard directed the marketing of Venesta, one of the leading plywood companies in Europe. It was inevitable then, that when Pritchard and Coates came to consider furnishings for the Lawn Road Flats, they took the opportunity to showcase the technological and aesthetic possibilities of plywood as part of their pioneering architectural proposition.

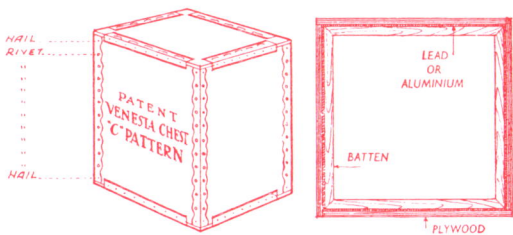

Tea chests to aircraft

The origins of Venesta, a contraction of 'Veneer and Estonia' are connected with a Scottish businessman E.H. Archer, a partner in a London firm shipping tea chests to plantations in Ceylon. Archer's enquiries to the A.M. Luther Company of Estonia, which had produced plywood boards since 1889, regarding the suitability of plywood for tea chests, led to a journey to Tallinn in 1895 to negotiate import arrangements.

←
Venesta Stool, c.1933. Probably manufactured in Estonia. Designer unknown.

The first plywood tea chests that Archer shipped to Ceylon proved to be very successful. The competitive edge of the product was secured by a waterproof glue that A.M. Luther had patented for plywood production. In 1897, the Venesta Syndicate Ltd was formed with exclusive rights to sell A.M. Luther plywood products in Britain and its colonies. Archer became the executive director and the founding members included the Luther brothers who also invested in the company. The formation of the international alliance led to a change in name of the A.M. Luther Company, it was re-branded Luterma.

Venesta's first years were dedicated to sales until, in 1900, riverside premises were bought in Limehouse to start the production of lead linings for tea chests. In 1907, with guidance from Luterma engineers, plywood production was set up in Millwall. These works, transferred to larger premises in Silvertown in 1910, proved of national importance during the First World War when large quantities of aeroply were produced for the aircraft industry.

Venesta-Luterma played a major role in the development of the European plywood industry. Owing to Venesta's marketing effort and exclusive rights, the early forms of plywood were commonly referred to as 'Venesta board'. By 1914 the companies had established branches in Finland, Germany, Holland, France and Italy.

→
Venesta Display stand, designed by Skinner and Tecton for the Building Exhibition 1934, Olympia, London.

Pritchard and plywood

During 1920–40, Venesta and Luterma were extending the range and variety of plywood products. Pritchard's role in Venesta's Building Uses Department was to promote new applications for plywood. His contributions included organising a series of competitions and commissioning successful exhibition stands from leading modernist designers Charlotte Perriand, Wells Coates, Francis Skinner of Tecton and Serge Chermayeff.

↑
With this 1929 design, Jack Pritchard demonstrated the use of *Plymax*, the new metal-faced plywood imported into Britain by Venesta. Affectionately described by Pritchard as 'the oven', the top of the cabinet is surfaced with stainless steel, and the sides and doors with copper; the back is of galvanised iron and the handles are brass. The cabinet is now on display at the V&A.

→
Drawing of the long chair by Marcel Breuer, from the chair patent

Bent plywood and Isokon

The advancement of bent plywood technologies during the 1930s brought plywood to the fore as a structural material in its own right. Its novelty value and machine-made aesthetics attracted the interest of progressive architects and designers who experimented with its largely unexploited technical possibilities in furniture design. Fascinated by these developments, Pritchard left Venesta in 1935 to set up the Isokon Furniture Company. Venesta agreed to invest in his new venture and the collaboration between the companies continued until the Second World War. Venesta sponsored many Isokon projects which promoted innovative uses of plywood; they provided expertise, prototyping and production support. Notably, these included the Isokon Long Chair by Marcel Breuer and Walter Gropius's innovative ideas for furniture based on prefabricated bent plywood forms.

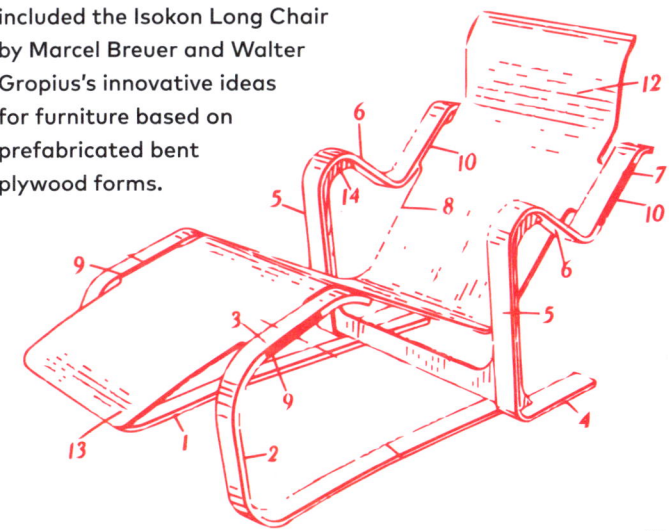

Isokon
The furniture

Christopher Wilk

Furniture was an integral part of the Pritchards' vision for the Isokon building. Jack's knowledge of plywood through his work with Venesta, combined with the arrival in London of Walter Gropius, lead to the creation of the Isokon Furniture Company, whose products have entered the canon of modern design.

Origins

Furniture was intended to be part of the Jack Pritchard–Wells Coates partnership from the beginning, even before the Isokon name was used. The concept for Lawn Road Flats explicitly envisioned the tenants as potential customers for Isokon furniture yet to be designed.

Walter Gropius's arrival in London in 1934 spurred Pritchard to create the Isokon Furniture Company with Gropius as Controller of Design. The aims of the new firm were announced in early 1936: to carry out research work as well as to undertake the designing and manufacture of furniture.

Given Pritchard's background in the plywood business it was no surprise that it was already decided that plywood was to be the principal material used in the first products.

←
Isokon trademark,
László Moholy-Nagy,
1936

An entirely new standard of comfort, and a further development of the English tradition of sound useful design, good workmanship and appropriate materials
Long chair brochure, 1936

Breuer and the Long Chair

Gropius suggested that his former Bauhaus colleague and protégé Marcel Breuer be hired to design furniture. Pritchard willingly agreed. At a first meeting between the three Gropius suggested that Breuer's first Isokon product should be a plywood reclining chair based closely on an aluminium chair Breuer had designed in 1932–33. Pritchard knew this chair well as he had purchased one in Switzerland in 1934 and used it in his Lawn Road flat.

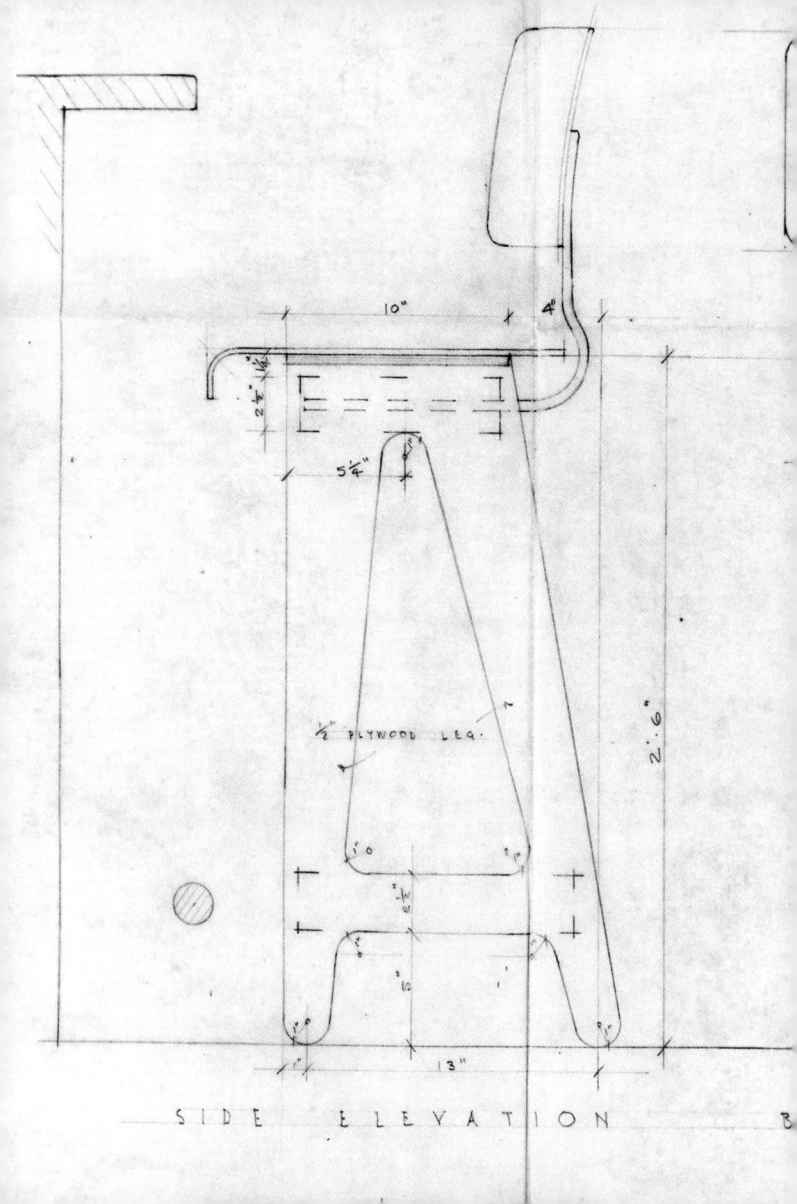

SIDE ELEVATION

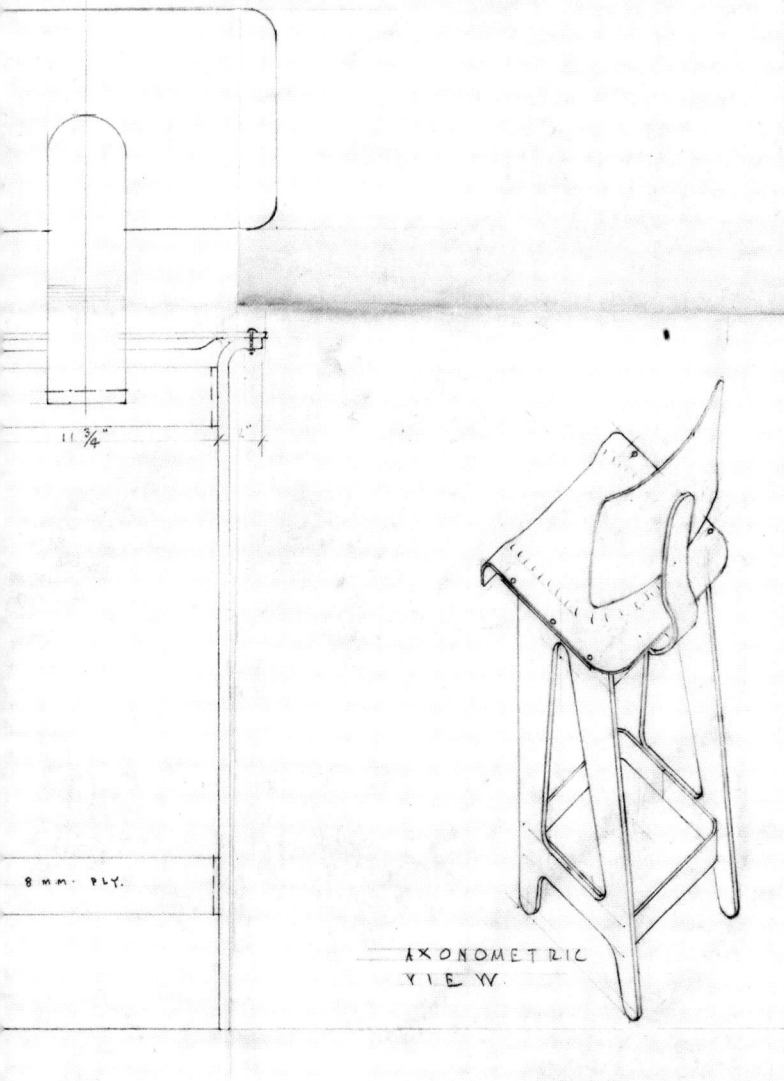

Plywood bar stool, Marcel Breuer, 1937

Breuer designed a range of furniture for Isokon which included a set of nesting tables, a square table and a dining table with stacking chairs. He also designed the Isobar, entirely furnished with Isokon furniture.

Gropius designed a number of plywood tables for Isokon, a pencil rack and a waste paper basket. Only the basket was manufactured, in aluminium by another firm. In 1937 Gropius and then Breuer left London to take up teaching positions at Harvard University in America.

Dining table and nesting tables, Marcel Breuer 1936

As a rule I am not in the habit of using superlatives, but I feel Breuer deserves them
Walter Gropius, 1937

→
Stacking dining chairs
Marcel Breuer, 1936

↓
Waste paper basket,
1935, side table GT2,
1936, by Walter Gropius

Bottleships and Donkeys

Émigré Austrian architect Egon Riss lived at Lawn Road Flats in 1939. Collaborating with Pritchard, Riss designed four small, innovative storage items: the Bottleship and Pocket Bottleship for bottles and glasses; the Gull for tabletop book storage; and the Penguin Donkey, designed to hold the recently introduced paperback Penguin books. The Donkey seemed destined for success after Penguin Books agreed to advertise with leaflets inserted into their books. However, after war broke out in September 1939, Isokon ended production.

← Pocket Bottleship, Egon Riss, 1939

→ Penguin Donkey, Egon Riss, 1939

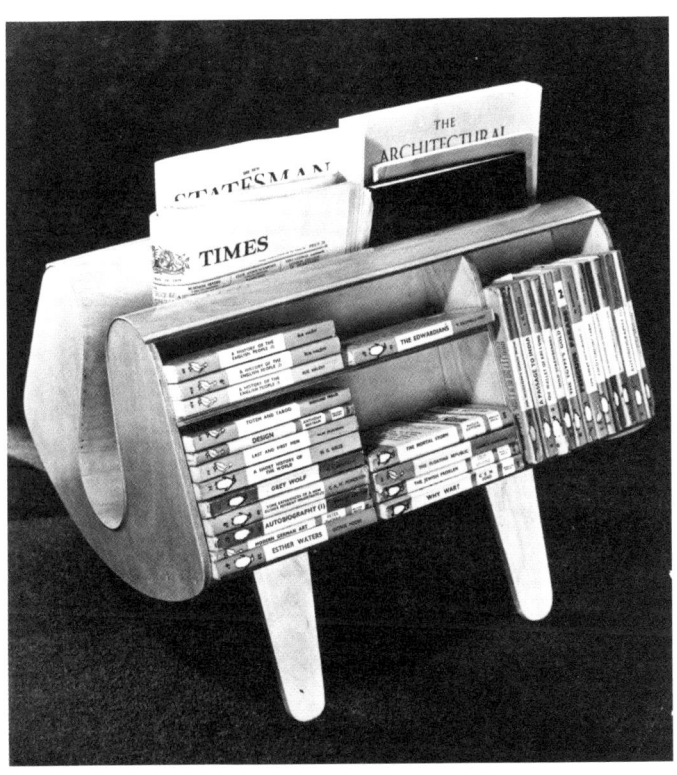

Pritchard attempted to revive the Isokon Furniture Company after the war, but only achieved this in 1963. The Long Chair was made in small quantities during the '60s as well as non-plywood versions of the Bottleship and Penguin Donkey, re-designed by Ernest Race. In 1982 Windmill Furniture – and from 1999 its Isokon Plus branch – have manufactured Isokon furniture under licence from the Pritchard family.

The Isokon Furniture Company was a very small, experimental and financially unprofitable venture. Nonetheless, its influential products have entered the canon of modern furniture.

←
Bottleship Mk II
Ernest Race, 1963

→
Penguin Donkey Mk II
Ernest Race, 1963

The Isobar
The social hub

John Allan

Designed by Marcel Breuer and F.R.S. Yorke and opened in 1937, this communal bar and restaurant in the Isokon attracted not only residents but a wide circle of artists and intellectuals from around Hampstead and beyond.

ISOKON MENU

Vegetable Soup
(Terror Afrorum)

Boiled Cod & Egg Sauce
(Bacalao con huevos)

Stewed Rabbit & Potatoes
(Lapin ivfe; Jamaica Potatoes)

Port Wine Type Jellies
(Just so)

Camp Coffee or none at all
(None at all, of course)

<u>Wines</u>
Rainwater
Chambertin 1923 bottled 1927
Tokay

Ingredients

The Isobar is another illustration of the Pritchards' gregarious and free-thinking nature. The central kitchen originally incorporated into the housekeeper's flat on the ground floor to provide meals for the residents upstairs had proved to be too large for the eventual demand, most tenants apparently preferring to prepare food in their own kitchens, despite their diminutive size. In its place therefore it was decided to create a communal bar and restaurant that could become a social focus for the Isokon building. Marcel Breuer, who had arrived in 1935, was commissioned to design the conversion and the Isobar was opened in 1937. Combining in its name the 'Iso' brand with Molly's obsession with the weather (a barograph being prominently installed for daily readings) the Isobar opened onto the rear terrace on the sunny side of the block allowing additional space for outdoor dining.

The new clubroom became an immediate success, attracting not only occupants of the building but a wide circle of artists and intellectuals from around Hampstead and beyond. Visitors included Ben Nicholson, Barbara Hepworth, Serge Chermayeff, Naum Gabo, Julian Huxley and others.

Following the sale of the building to the New Statesman newspaper in 1969, the Isobar was removed and the space converted into residential use.

←
Isobar menu, c.1937

↑
Isobar restaurant, featuring pictures of Breuer, Kenwood House and a map of North West London

→
Isobar hearth area, featuring a barometer and current surface pressure chart

←
Philip Harben, Isobar chef

Half-Hundred Club

The Isobar was closely associated with the Half Hundred Club, also founded by Jack Pritchard and others in 1937 as a 'poor man's food and wine society'. The club had 25 members each of whom could bring one guest, hence the half hundred. Its aim was to combine good dining with economy. A budget restriction of ten shillings for members and guests (inclusive of food, wine and service) was imposed, with any overspend being made up at the host's expense. Members took turns to direct a dinner which could involve simply planning the menu and having someone else cook it, or alternatively buying the food and wine, cooking the meal and serving it. An advance 'blurb' was required to be circulated and any members who failed to confirm their attendance would be charged an impoliteness fee. Other membership rules stipulated that acceptance of new members should be by unanimous vote and that guests should possess *no religious or other taboos or unsociable characteristics which may impede conversation*. Diners were also served in strict rotation *without distinction of sex or other favouritism*.

Although many of the dinners were cooked and held in the Pritchards' penthouse, on occasion the dinners were held further afield, venues including a Chinese restaurant, a cinema, and London Zoo. Key figures in the Club, besides Pritchard, Harben and Huxley (whose dinner at the Zoo featured bison's tail, locally sourced) included Francis Meynell and Raymond Postgate, later founding author of The Good Food Guide. The club ceased its activities in 1940 although there was a brief revival after World War II.

RULES OF THE HALF HUNDRED CLUB

1. The Club shall be known as the Half Hundred, and shall consist of not more than 25 members, each of whom shall have the right to bring one guest. The object of the Club is to combine good dining with economy.

2. Members other than foundation members must be proposed and seconded by existing members. No member may propose his or her wife or husband and no candidate shall be proposed who has not previously attended at least one dinner as a guest. Members must be elected nem. con. and a member proposing a candidate must certify him or her to be seriously and intelligently interested in food and drink and to possess no religious or other taboos or unsociable characteristics which may impede conversation. No person wholly or principally employed in the wine or food trade shall be eligible for membership, but existing members who enter these trades shall not be asked to resign.

3. Ten dinners shall be held yearly. No entrance or membership fee shall be charged but each member shall pledge himself to attend and/or pay for not less than six dinners, whose maximum permissible cost he shall pay for in advance. The total price for any meal shall not exceed 5/- per head for food, 4/6 for wine, and 6d. for service. Except when dinner is given at a restaurant the price of raw food materials shall not exceed 2/6. Smoking is not permitted until the dinner is over, and members are desired to call their guests' attention to this rule.

4. Every dinner shall be planned and supervised by a member, who may also cook it if he so desires; every member must be willing and competent to direct such a dinner; and members shall be selected for this duty in rotation. Volunteers shall be called for first; upon these failing the director shall be selected by lot from those who have not already served. On the list of members being exhausted the process shall be resumed. The director shall preside at the dinner and shall deliver to the secretary not less than a week beforehand a blurb or anticipatory account of the meal, to be circulated to members.

5. Every member shall notify the secretary on receipt of the blurb whether he is attending, failing which he shall be charged the cost of the food, a fair proportion of the wine and 2/- Impoliteness Fee. No meal shall be delayed for late arrivals and diners shall be served in strict rotation without distinction of sex or other favouritism.

6. Dinners may be provided at the director's discretion at a private house, a restaurant, or Lawn Road Flats. In the last-named case he shall organise the meal in collaboration with the chef whom he shall approach not less than 3 days before the meal and Isokon will provide the service, cooking, crockery and room charging for this a sum twice the cost of raw materials excluding wine.

7. Until otherwise decided the secretary shall be J. C. Pritchard who with 3 other duly elected members shall constitute the Executive Committee of the Club.

Hampstead in the 1930s

Alan Powers

Home to culturally progressive people of all professions, Hampstead garnered a reputation as the intellectual and reforming centre of London during the 1930s

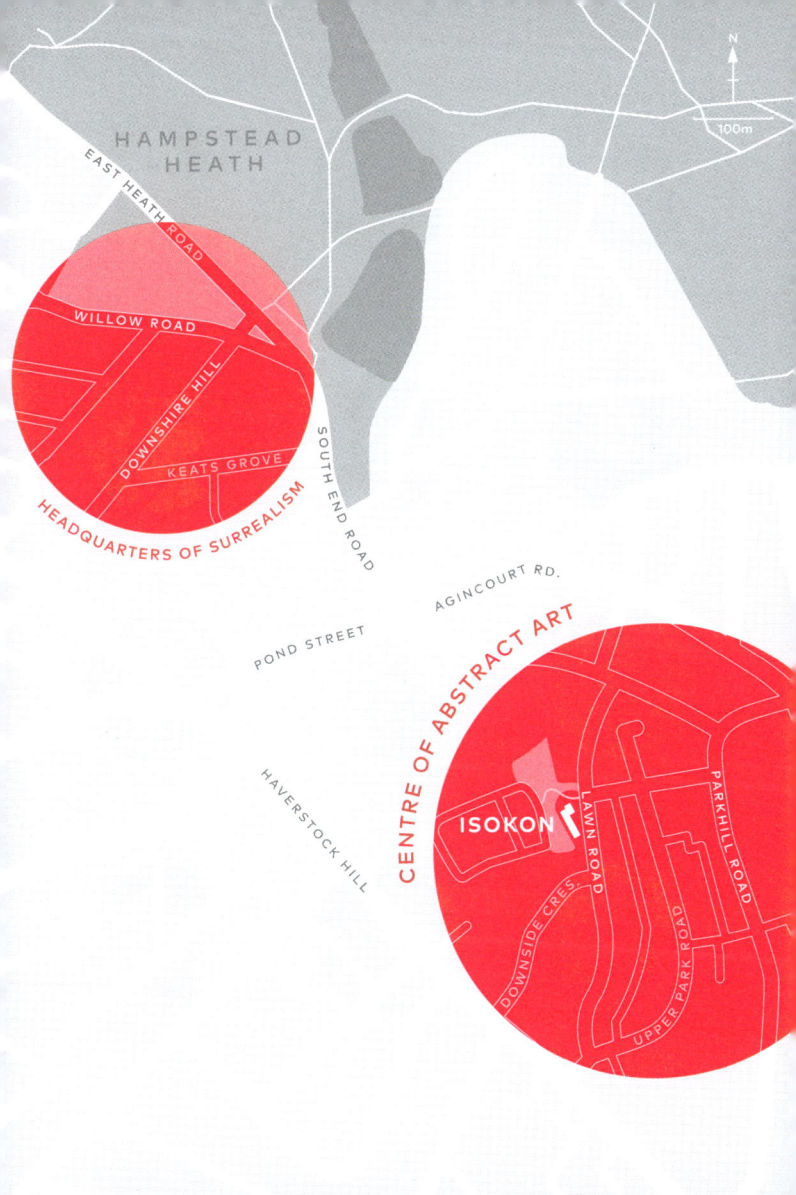

Roland Penrose
Artist

Lee Miller
Photographer

J.D. Bernal
Scientist

Margaret Gardiner
Artist

Fred Uhlman
Artist

Oskar Kokoschka
Artist

John Heartfield
Artist

Ernő Goldfinger
Architect

Berthold Lubetkin
Architect

Anna Freud
Psychoanalyst

Mark Gertler
Artist

George Orwell
Writer

Hampstead in the 1930s represents a time and place like Chelsea in the 1890s or Bloomsbury and Hammersmith in the 1920s. Each of these locations had old houses that were characterful and comparatively cheap to rent or buy, in contrast to today. Lacking river views, Hampstead has its Heath, a natural landscape rather than a park, saved from development by public action in the 1860s.

Downshire Hill and Willow Road

Writers and artists were clustered in different parts of the borough. The home of the Carline family of artists at Nº47 Downshire Hill was a significant nucleus from 1916, while later residents in the street included Roland Penrose and photographer Lee Miller at Nº21 (making it the unofficial London headquarters of Surrealism), and the left-wing scientist J.D. Bernal at Nº35, with his partner, Margaret Gardiner. The German émigré artist, Fred Uhlman and his English wife, Diana, then bought Nº47. They were among the many local artists and intellectuals who worked to help German and Austrian artists escape from Berlin, Vienna and Prague, including Oskar Kokoschka and other Expressionist painters. The political collagist John Heartfield came to the Uhlmans for a weekend and stayed for three years. Just round the corner in Willow Road, Ernő and Ursula Goldfinger built their house in the centre of its terrace in 1938. Berthold Lubetkin, in whose Highpoint block the Goldfingers lived before this, founded his Tecton partnership at the Chiantor Restaurant in Hampstead in 1932.

Parkhill Road and Lawn Road

What Herbert Read called the 'nest of gentle artists' in the area of Parkhill Road resulted from the conjunction of Henry and Irina Moore at one end of the road with Barbara Hepworth and Ben Nicholson in the Mall Studios at the other end, joined by Read himself. With Paul Nash (resident in Eldon Road at the end of the decade), they were the nucleus of the Unit One group who banded together to exhibit in 1934. An older abstract artist, Cecil Stephenson, was already established there, and Hepworth and Nicholson arranged for Piet Mondrian to rent the ground floor of Nº60 in 1939–40. Briefly, this modest corner could claim to be the world centre of abstract art, with the Lawn Road Flats most appropriately its near neighbour, and a further group within easy distance, including Naum Gabo and László Moholy-Nagy in Golders Green. This community mostly dispersed at the beginning of the war.

Literary figures included the editor of *New Verse*, Geoffrey Grigson in Keats Grove, and poet Stephen Spender. The Everyman Cinema, opened in 1933, offered new foreign films and small foyer exhibitions of modern art, including the first in Britain of Paul Klee.

Geoffrey Grigson
Artist

Stephen Spender
Poet

Henry Moore
Artist

Barbara Hepworth
Artist

Ben Nicholson
Artist

Herbert Read
Artist

Cecil Stephenson
Artist

Paul Nash
Artist

Piet Mondrian
Artist

Naum Gabo
Artist

Towards a better future

Tensions existed between abstractionists and surrealists, and between different shades of political conviction, but all were united in wanting a better society for the future, confident that this could be achieved by harnessing technology, expanding public ownership of industry and infrastructure, and questioning if not discarding the cultural forms of the past.

If a few of the most prominent 1930s residents moved on, many more stayed to maintain Hampstead's reputation as the intellectual and reforming centre of London for several decades after the war.

A hotbed of spies
The secret history

Jill Pearlman

The Soviet spies found the modernist Lawn Road Flats an amenable place to live and ply their trade. Between 1935 and 1942, four spies working actively on behalf of the Soviet Union made it their home.

Isokon intelligence

Between 1935 and 1942, four spies working actively on behalf of the Soviet Union made their home in the Lawn Road Flats: Arnold Deutsch (1903–1942?), Simon Kremer (1899–1991), Jürgen Kuczynski (1904–97) and Brigitte Kuczynski Lewis (1910–97). Like so many Hampstead residents in this era, all four spies were Jewish by birth, Central European, and true believers in Stalin's idealised vision of the worker and the proletariat state.

Edith Tudor-Hart likely brought the first of the tenant-spies, Arnold Deutsch, into the building. She knew Deutsch from her native Vienna, and it was he who had recruited her into the NKVD (forerunner of the KGB) in 1934. Resident in the Flats from 1935 to 1936, Deutsch's legacy looms large in the history of Soviet intelligence. He recruited more than twenty British spies, most famously Kim Philby and others of the notorious Cambridge Five. The espionage ring of young Cambridge graduates would pass vast amounts of classified intelligence to the Soviets for nearly twenty years.

The second Lawn Road spy, Simon Kremer, rented his Isokon flat from 1936 to 1938. While in London, he worked for the Soviets as a recruiter and controller, the person to whom the spies report. Together with the third spy in the Lawn Road Flats, Jürgen Kuczynski, Kremer played a key role in the famous case of Klaus Fuchs, the German-born English physicist who handed on highly classified information about the atomic bomb.

Arnold Deutsch
Isokon resident 1935–6
Recruited numerous spies: Edith Tudor-Hart, Kim Philby and the rest of the Cambridge Five.

Simon Kremer
Isokon resident 1936–7
Soviet spy recruiter and controller, key role in the case of Klaus Fuchs, who supplied the Soviet Union with atomic bomb secrets.

Brigitte Kuczynski Lewis
Isokon resident 1937–41
Assisted her sister Ursula, a renowned GRU agent codenamed 'Sonya', by recruiting agents to work clandestinely for the Soviet Union in Nazi Germany.

Jürgen Kuczynski
Isokon resident 1940–42
Secretary of the exiled German Communists in London. Passed information to Soviet intelligence and helped his sister Ursula.

Edith Tudor-Hart
Tudor-Hart had close ties to the Isokon. A Bauhaus-trained photographer and friend of Jack and Molly, she knew it well having photographed the flats for them.

Kim Philby
Recruited by Arnold Deutsch, Philby was a member of the spy ring now known as the Cambridge Five; believed to have been the most successful in providing secret information to the Soviet Union.

Eva Collet Reckitt
Isokon resident 1940–42
Owner of the Communist bookshop Collet's in Charing Cross Road. Described by MI5 as 'the Communist Party's milch-cow'

Kuczynski lived in the Flats between 1940 and 1941. A distinguished economic historian and leader of German Communists in London during the Nazi era, he often passed important information to the Soviets via his eldest sister. Code-named 'Sonya', Ruth Kuczynski was one of the most decorated female spies in the history of Soviet espionage. Though Sonya never lived in the Lawn Road Flats, a younger sister, Brigitte Kuczynski Lewis, lived there between 1936 and 1942. Brigitte too delivered classified information to the Soviets and helped Sonya recruit new spies.

Hiding in plain sight

The Soviet spies found the modernist Lawn Road Flats an amenable place to live and ply their trade for several reasons. Above all, they blended inconspicuously into the sociable community of residents here. Many tenants too were refugees from Central Europe, most left-leaning and also transient, living only a short time in their 'ready-to-live-in' flats. The spies could also 'hide in plain sight' in the surrounding neighbourhoods, home in the 1930s and 40s to a vast community of European refugees.

Even the Lawn Road Flats building worked well for the spies. One could enter and exit any unit discreetly, and with their small windows on the street side, no one could see in. At the same time, the cantilevered decks on each floor provided the tenant-spies a perfect vantage point from which to survey the street below.

Ruin & rescue
The restoration

John Allan

The Isokon is a building that epitomised progressive ideas of city living 80 years ago, and has become modern again, thanks to a restoration project undertaken by Notting Hill Housing Group that was completed in 2004.

Social vision

In the post-war years, as a result of changes in ownership and inadequate maintenance, the building deteriorated and eventually became uninhabitable, even giving rise to doubts over its survival.

Isokon rear entrance, c.2000, in a state of dereliction

In collaboration with Notting Hill Housing Group and The Isokon Trust, a team led by Avanti Architects won a competition sponsored by Camden Council in 2000 to acquire, conserve, and regenerate the apartment block. The team believed that with the right social vision and appropriate technical intervention the Isokon could once again be made a viable and desirable place to live. Notting Hill's commitment to keyworker housing, shared ownership and mixed tenure sustainable development was an important factor in winning the bid. Meanwhile the architectural objective was that the rescue work should be underpinned by an informed conservation philosophy that honoured the original significance of the design, while also addressing the necessity for major repair and upgrade work.

Resuscitation

The building as found was in a dire state. Much of the original fabric had been lost, was covered up or unsympathetically altered. But forensic site investigation and the extensive documentary sources that survived provided the references needed to establish both the authentic design and also offered pointers to the correct response where a new intervention was needed.

   The works comprised comprehensive rehabilitation of the reinforced concrete envelope and restoration of the original façade colour (a pale pink); replacement of asphalt membranes, major upgrade of insulation values; renewal of wall, ceiling and floor finishes, windows and doors; refurbishment of light metalwork elements and fitted joinery wherever possible, and replacement to match original where not. Whilst the original plan layout of the units has been retained throughout, minute dimensional adjustments were made to accommodate new requirements such as refrigerators and washing machines. Mechanical and electrical services were completely re-engineered to comply with current standards, but in such a way as to be consistently disciplined by architectural conservation constraints - likewise the integration of new communication, signage and security installations. The site curtilage was also fully rehabilitated with a scheme of external works and soft landscaping.

←
Bathroom and kitchen,
pre- and post-rescue

Partition wall moved 100mm, enabling fridge to be introduced into kitchen

Dressing room redesigned to include washing machine (shaded area)

Cupboard behind WC encloses combi boiler

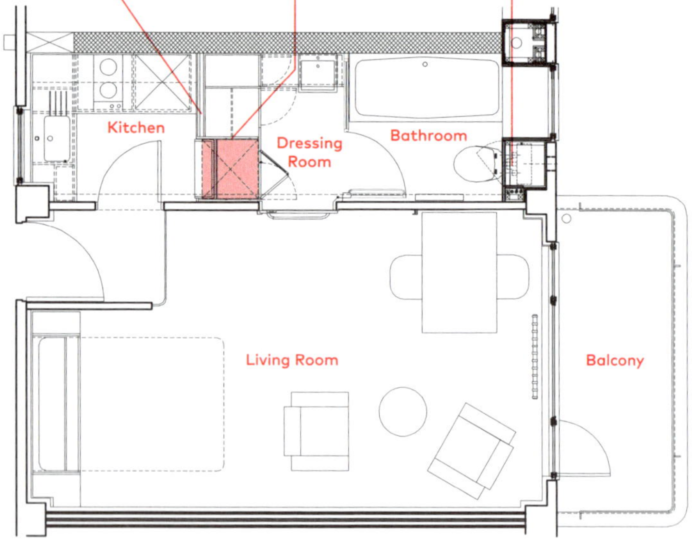

Kitchen

Dressing Room

Bathroom

Living Room

Balcony

↑
Interventions to minimum flat

→
Restored one-bed flat

Revival

The Isokon restoration has provided 25 flats under shared ownership for keyworkers, while eleven further flats were sold on the open market. Although it was not possible to reinstate the Isobar (which had already been converted into flats in 1970) consent was obtained to convert the former garage into the Isokon Gallery exhibition space to present the history of the building and promote understanding of the radical ideas behind its creation. The Gallery was opened in 2014.

Summary specification

Roof
The existing defective roof coverings were entirely removed back to the concrete slab, and concrete repair carried out. New tapered cellular glass insulation was laid to improved falls with channels and reformed rainwater outlets followed by the application of polymer modified asphalt coverings and promenade paviors.

Windows and doors
The non-original windows were replaced to the original fenestration pattern and colour with W40 double glazed, low E, argon filled, and polyester powder coated steel windows. Doors were renewed within the original cast-in steel doorframes, which have been retained and repaired in situ.

Internal partitions
The internal layout of the original apartments was retained, with separating walls being acoustically upgraded and internal partitions replaced with metal stud plasterboard partitions.

External Walls
The numerous accumulated layers of paint and cementitious coatings were removed to re-establish the original concrete face. Survey work was undertaken to determine the extent of latent as well as patent damage. Concrete repair and local replacement was followed by application of fairing coats and elastomeric anti-carbonation coating to the original building colour. The imprint of original shuttering lines was retained, and a small area showing the succession of over coatings during the 80-year life of the building is displayed below the escape stair as an historical record. The internal faces of the external walls, originally cork but severely deteriorated, were cleaned, repaired and lined with thermal laminate board and skimmed to achieve current insulation values.

Services

The previous (non-original) communal heating system with its external surface mounted pipework was removed and new gas fired individually controlled combination boilers were installed, thereby avoiding the impact of a hot water storage tank on the internal plan arrangement of the flats, and eliminating the need for an on-site electricity sub station. The balanced flue terminals were specially designed to be contained within the building line in the original vent grille openings.

Fittings

The closely detailed kitchen, dressing room and bathroom areas were reconstructed in accordance with the original Wells Coates' design but upgraded to incorporate household appliances to meet with current standards. Surviving viable internal original plywood fittings were carefully removed, stored, restored and reinstated where possible. Linings, floors and sliding panels, including the ply paneling and fittings in Jack Pritchard's penthouse were restored by the cabinetry specialist Nick Goldfinger, with matching pieces being introduced to make good missing fragments. Surviving original Well Coates designed 'D' handles were restored and recoated.

Isokon restored, 2004

Chronology

1933 Oct   Construction of Lawn Road Flats commences

1934 Jul   Completion and formal opening

1937 Nov   The Isobar opens, designed by Marcel Breuer

1969 Jan   Lawn Road Flats sold to the *New Statesman*

1970   Planning application to convert Isobar into flats

1972   Sold to Camden Council, renamed Isokon Flats

1974 May   Listed Grade II by English Heritage

1979   Windows replaced

1999   Listed Grade I by English Heritage

2001 Feb   Notting Hill Housing Group / Avanti Architects team win competition to regenerate building

2003 May   Work commences on site

2004 Dec   Project completion

2014 Jul   Isokon Gallery opens

2018 Jul   English Heritage Blue Plaque unveiled

Further reading

Isokon and the Bauhaus in Britain
Leyla Daybelge and Magnus Englund (Batsford, 2019)
ISBN 978-1849944915

Belsize 2000 – a living suburb
(The Belsize Conservation Area Advisory Committee, 2000)
ISBN 0-953942104

Isokon
Alastair Grieve, essay in *Modern Britain 1929–1939* (Design Museum, 1999)
ISBN 978-1843837831

Lawn Road Flats: Spies, Writers and Artists
David Burke (Boydell Press, 2014)
ISBN 978-1843837831

Modern – The Modern Movement in Britain
Alan Powers (Merrell, 2007)
ISBN 978-1858944050

The Door to a Secret Room: A Portrait of Wells Coates
Laura Cohn – daughter of Wells Coates (Ashgate Publishing, 1999)
ISBN 978-1840146950

View From a Long Chair
Jack Pritchard (Law Book Co. of Australasia, 1984)
ISBN 978-0710202314

Wells Coates
Elizabeth Darling (RIBA, 2012)
ISBN 978-1859464373

Wells Coates: a monograph
Sherban Cantacuzino (Gordon Fraser Gallery, 1978)
ISBN 978-0900406591

Image credits

Page	Credit
Cover	Isokon Gallery logo based on a drawing by Wells Coates
3–9	Tom de Gay
10–15, 47, 55 (bottom), 56–59, 62, 67	Pritchard Archives, University of East Anglia
16	Laura Cohn collection
21, 27, 29, 31, 33, 34, 41, 52	RIBA Library Drawings Collection
22	Unknown Photographer. Collection of Canadian Centre for Architecture (CCA)
23 (top), 42	Victoria & Albert Museum
23 (bottom)	Magnus Englund
24, 30, 37	Edith Tudor-Hart
32, 35, 45	RIBA Library Photographs Collection
38, 48	Philip Harben
39	Lelikron/Wikipedia
40	Lucia Moholy
46, 54, 55 (top)	Dan Tsantilis, Victoria & Albert Museum
51	Skandium
60, 64 (top), 65	Dell & Wainwright / RIBA Collections
78, 79, 80 (top), 82	Avanti Architects
80 (bottom), 83	Robert Gresshof
86	Nick Kane
92	Facsimilie of plaque in the Isokon's entrance lobby, unveiled on 9 July 2014

The Isokon Gallery is generously supported by

ARAM STORE — artek — ATRIVM — AVANTI ARCHITECTS

conisbee — CWM — CUBITTS — Haines Watts

HERITAGE FUND — Historic England — ISOKON PLUS — iittala

GUBI — MARGARET HOWELL — MAX FORDHAM — MOOMIN

Paul Smith — Praxis — Penguin — RIBA

SCP — SHARPE PRITCHARD — Sigma Roc — SKANDIUM

ske — stace — THE MODERN HOUSE ESTATE AGENTS — THE MOHOLY-NAGY FOUNDATION

vitra. — VITSŒ

JONATHAN & MARIA PRITCHARD & FAMILY
PAUL & MARC FELLERMAN
CHRIS & LONE MCCOURT
ANDREW PERLOFF

MATTHEW & SUSANNA WELLS COHN
RICHARD ROGERS
MAX JANKEL STERNE
DAVID USBORNE

THE ISOKON BUILDING

LAWN ROAD FLATS

**OPENED
9 JULY 1934**

◆ ARCHITECT · WELLS COATES ◆

CLIENT · JACK & MOLLY PRITCHARD
OWNER · NOTTING HILL HOUSING GROUP
GRADE I LISTED BY ENGLISH HERITAGE 1999
RESTORATION · AVANTI ARCHITECTS 2004